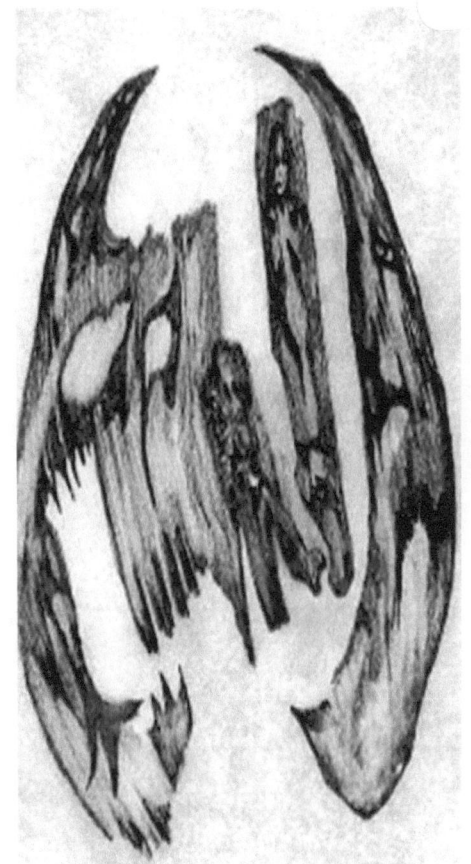

Ying and Yang

Copyright 2012 December

Ron Koppelberger Jr.

Surreal Dreams Two

***

Websites

Wolffray.blogspot.com
Farthermostdream.blogspot.com
Horrorrush.blogspot.com
Mirageinblame.blogspot.com
Ravenswont.blogspot.com
Snakefuss.blogspot.com
Ethrealsouls.blogspot.com

Welcome

Enjoy The Show

(Dreams will be served afterward)

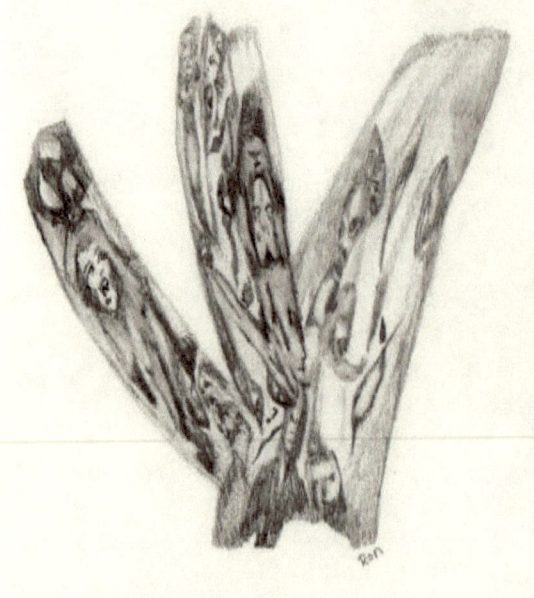

Three Paths

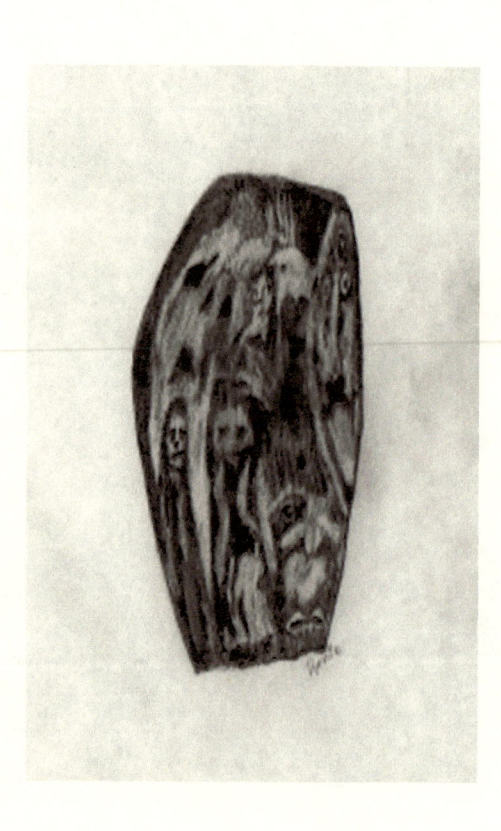

The Woods Around Me

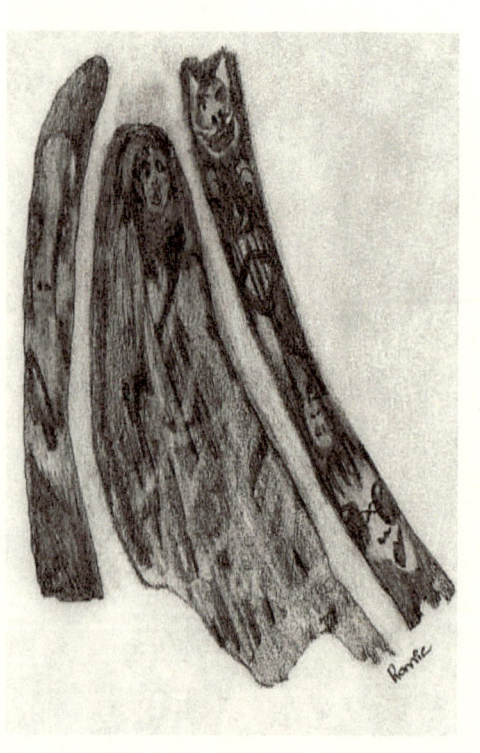

Forward and Backward

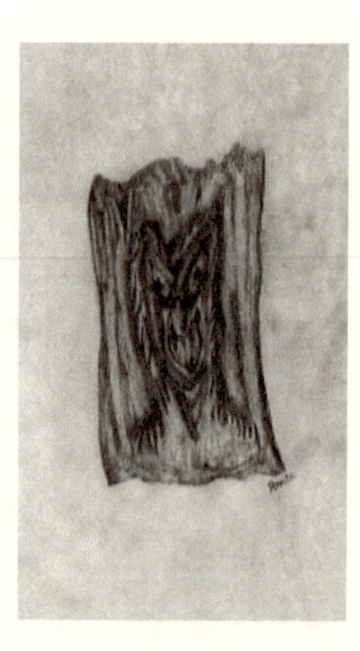

A Devil

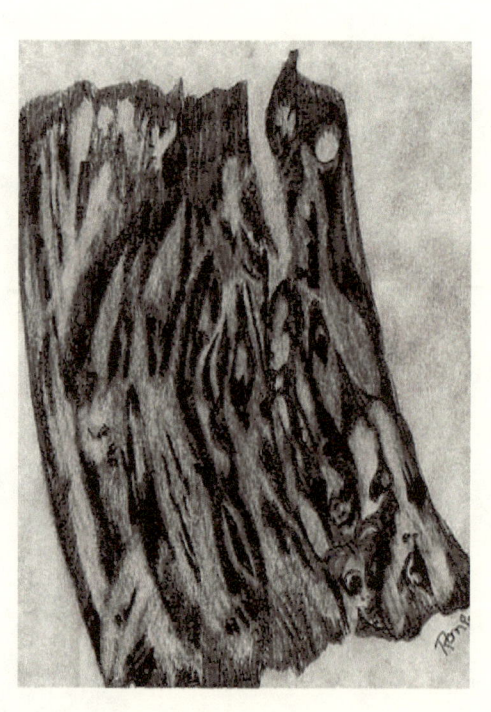

Morphing

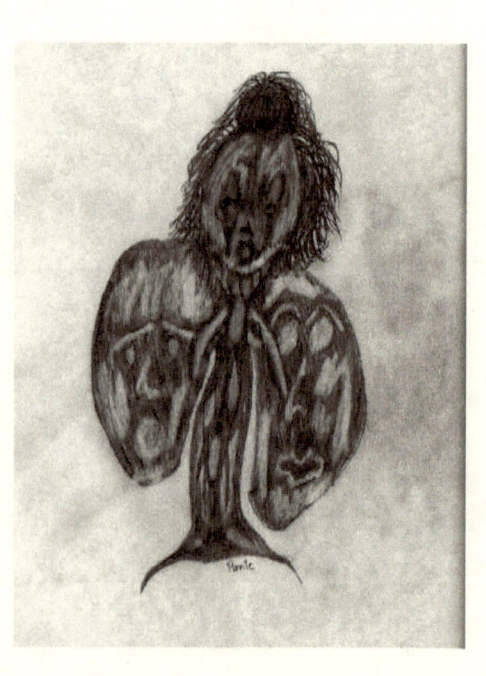

She Finds The Night

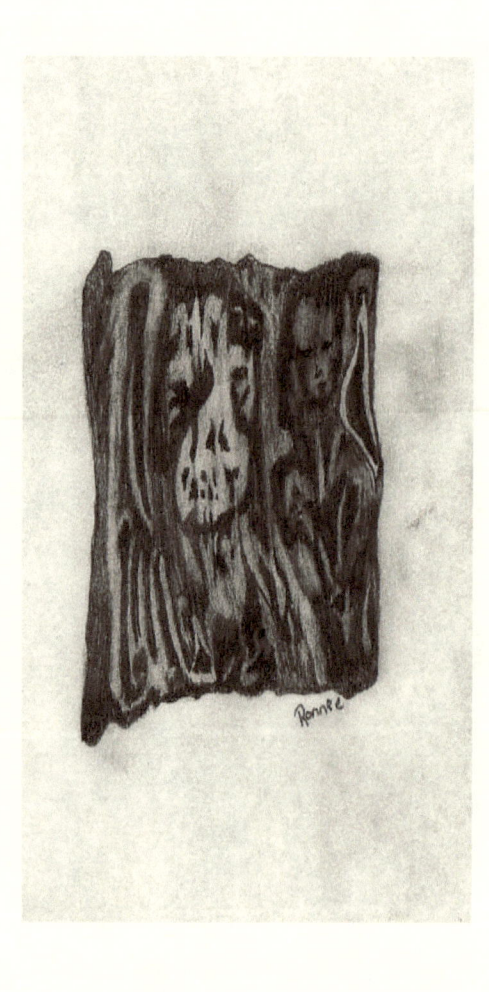

The Queen Of Shadows

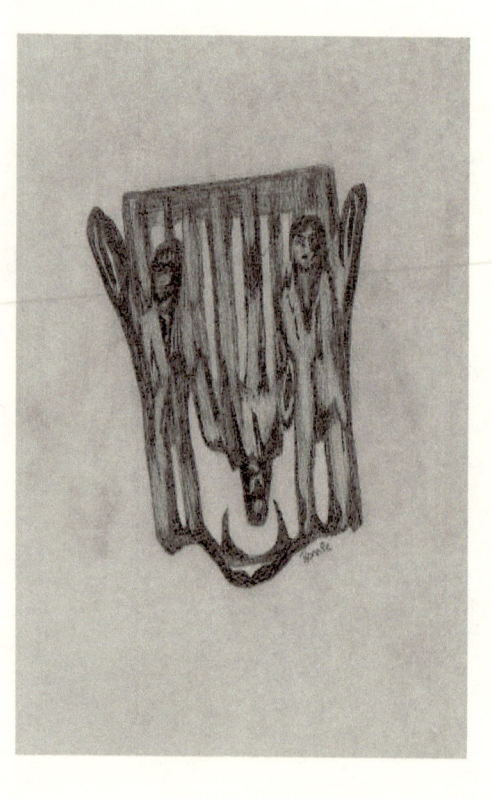

The Three

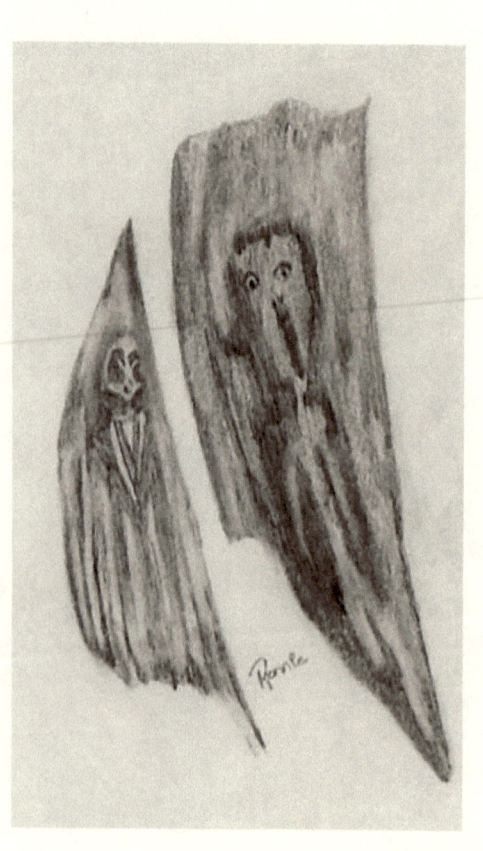

She Screams

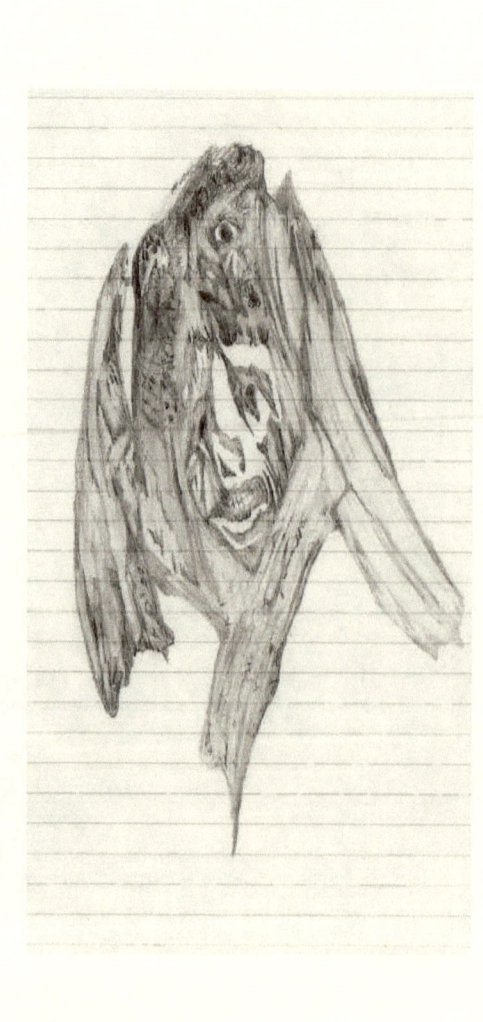

Finding The Way

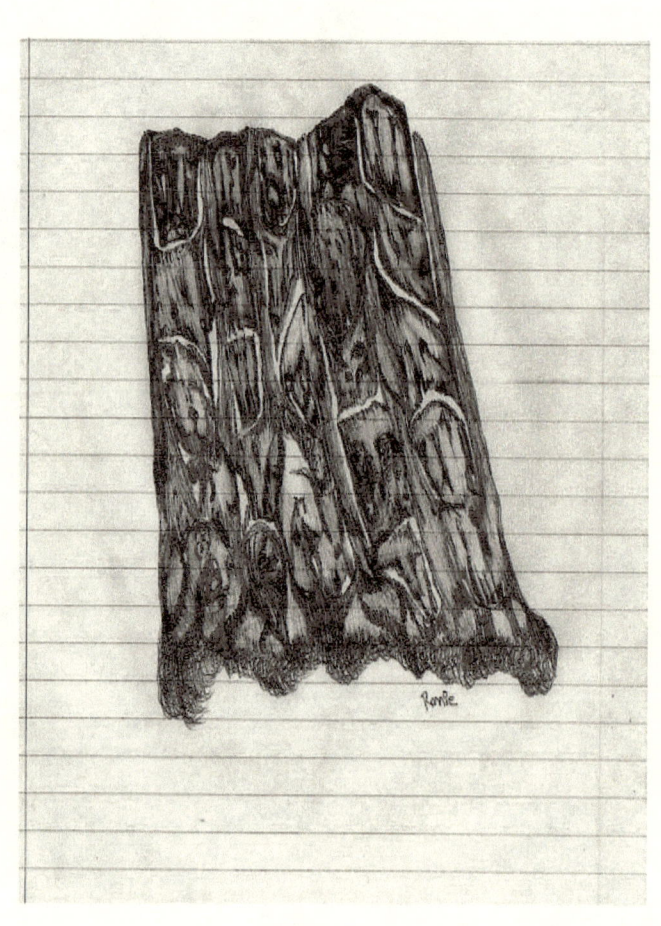

The Stump In Secret

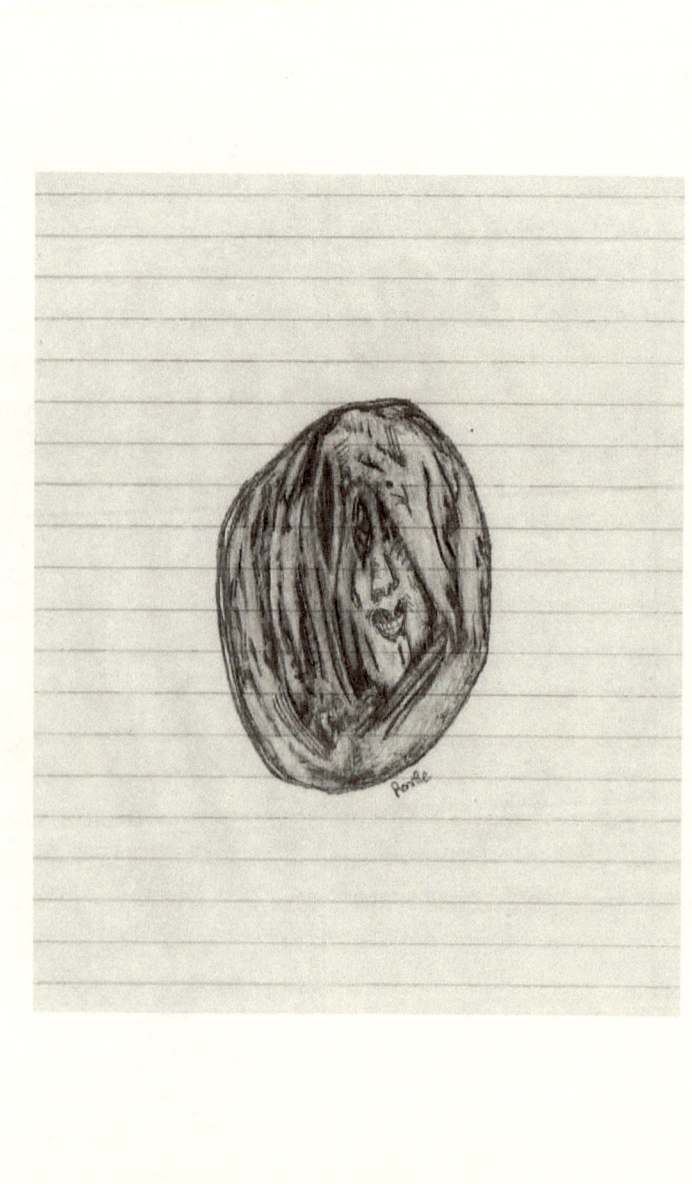

The Monk

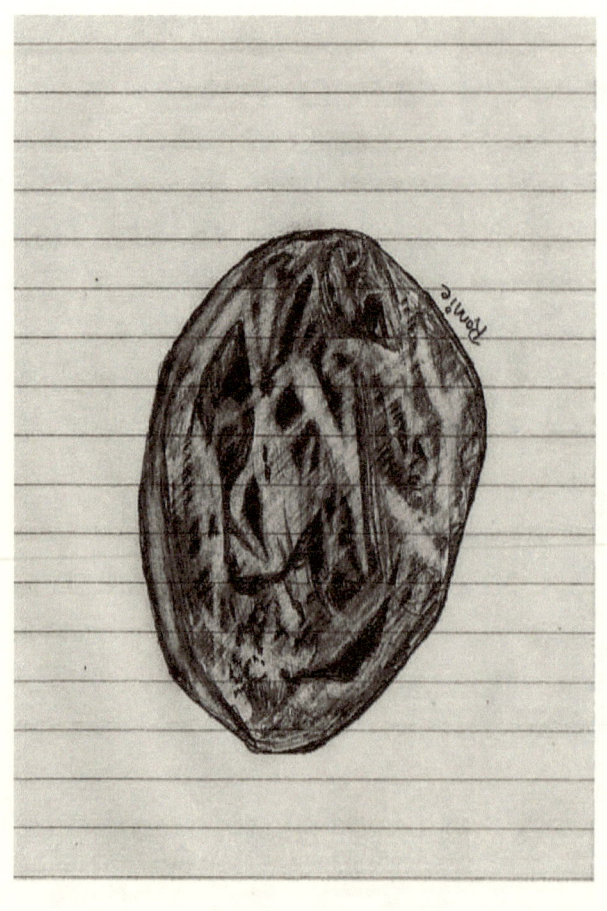

Jumbled Images of Fate

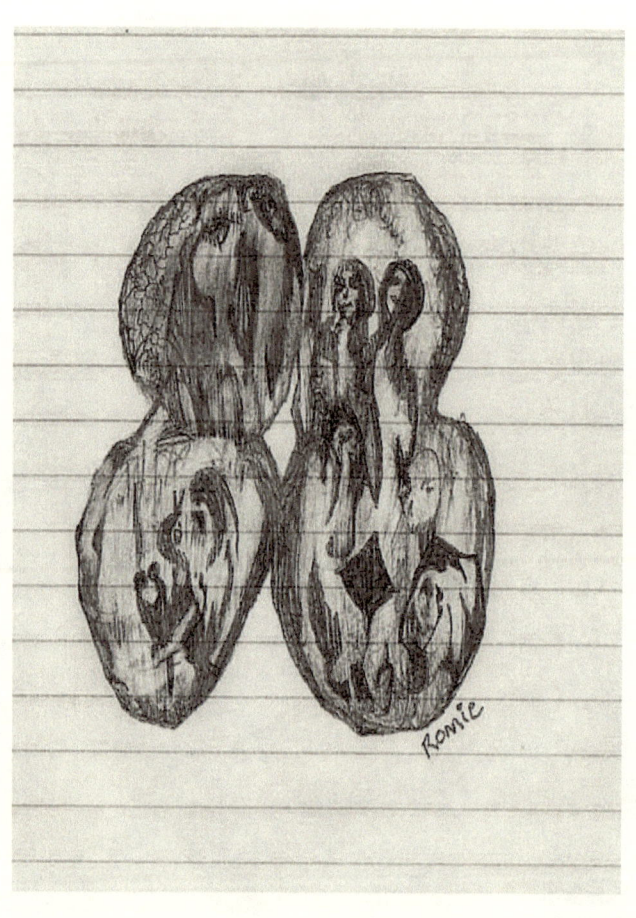

Four Globes

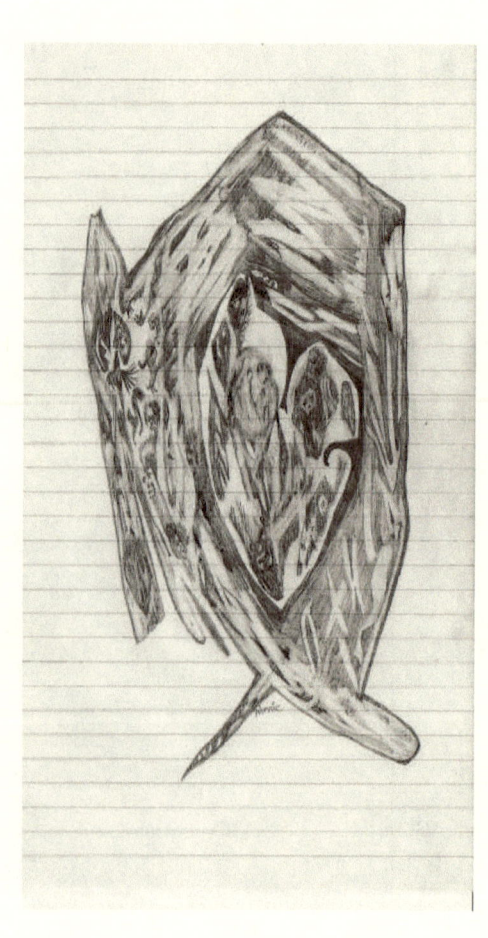

Full Circle

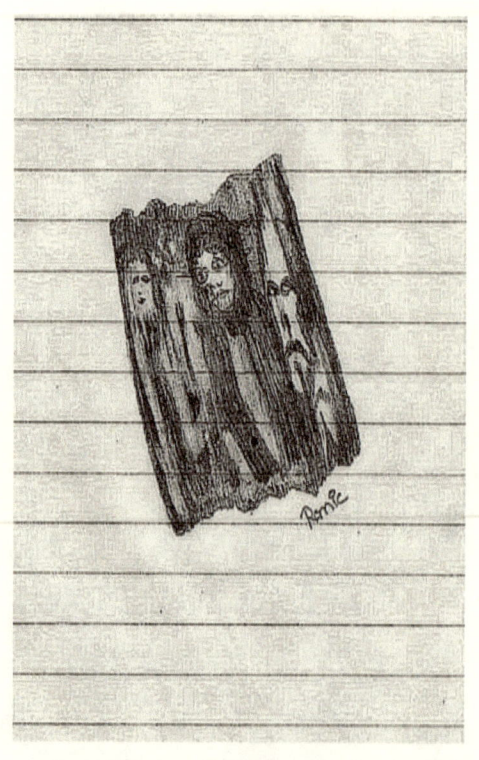

Facing The Door

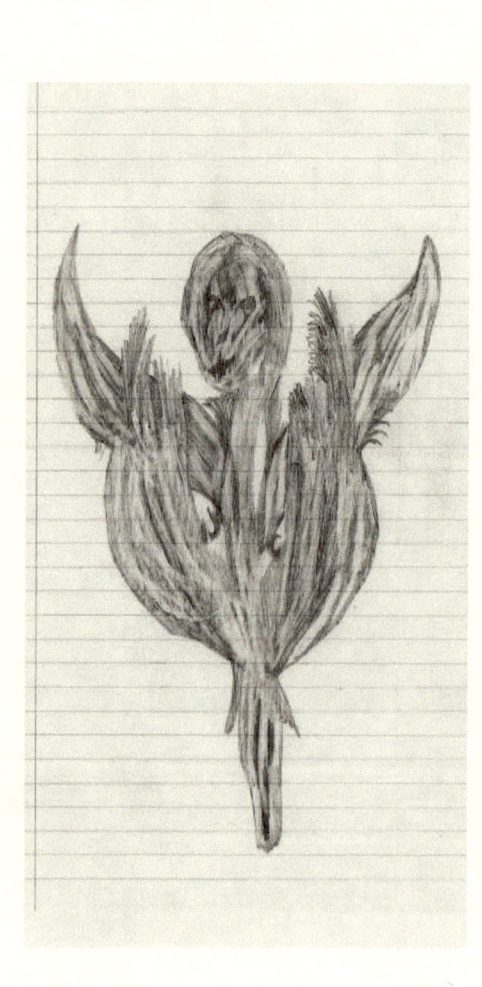

The Bird

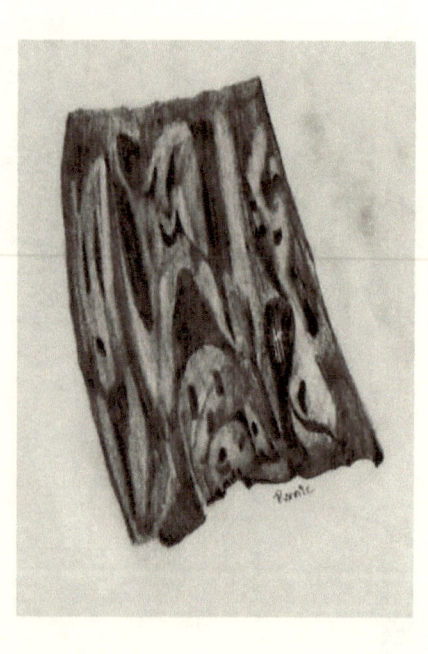

Ghosts

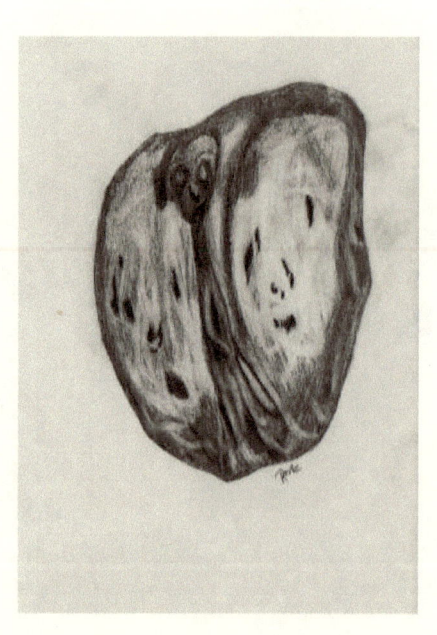

Jus Passin Through

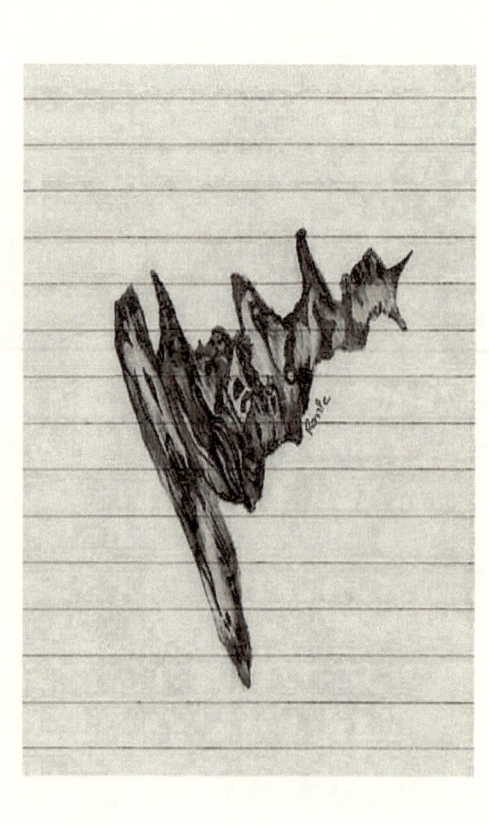

Segmented

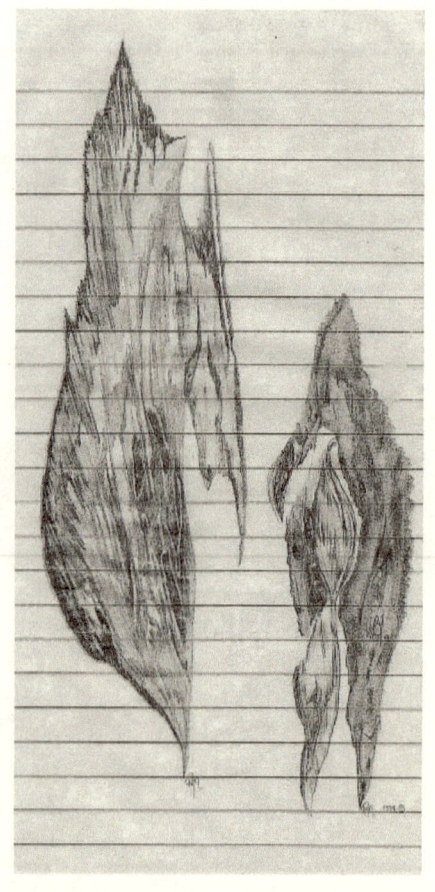

Asking the Sage

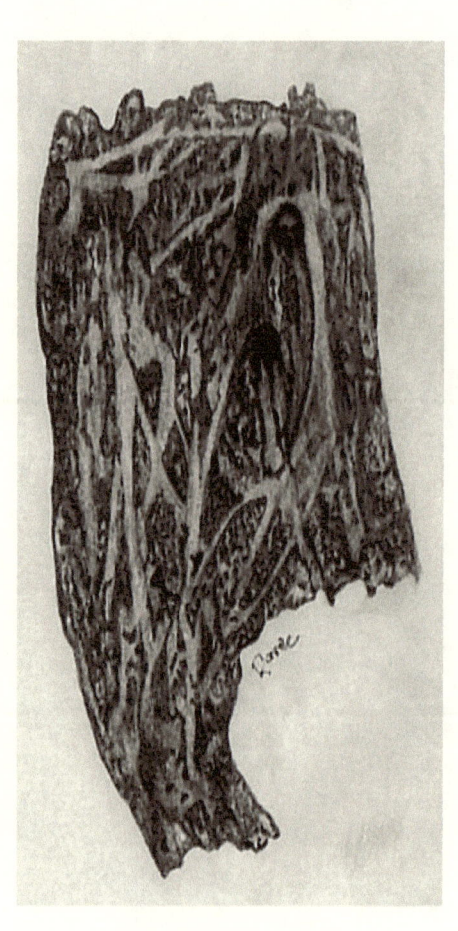

Metamorphosis

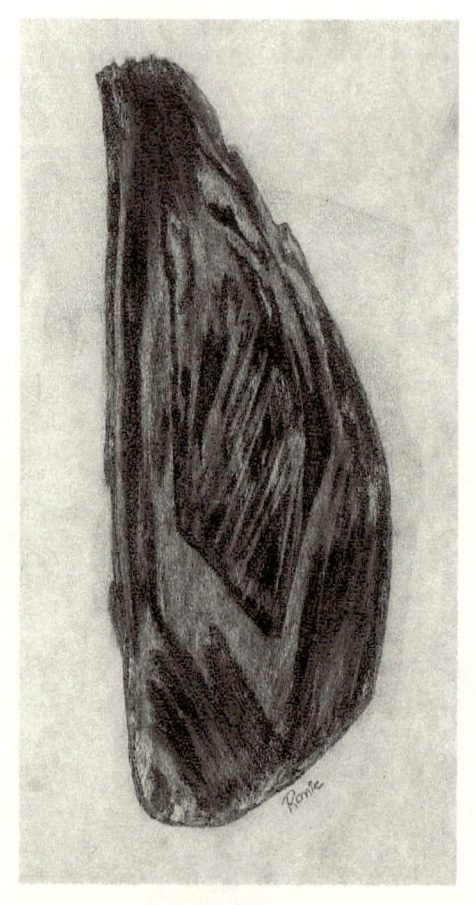

The Mummy

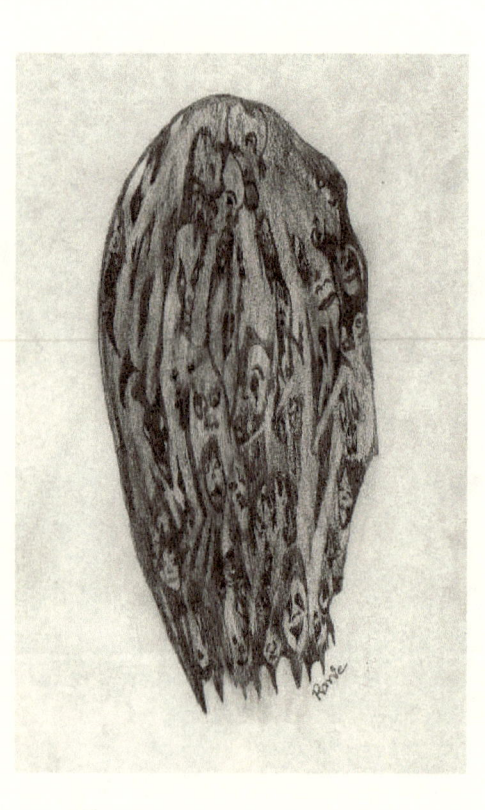

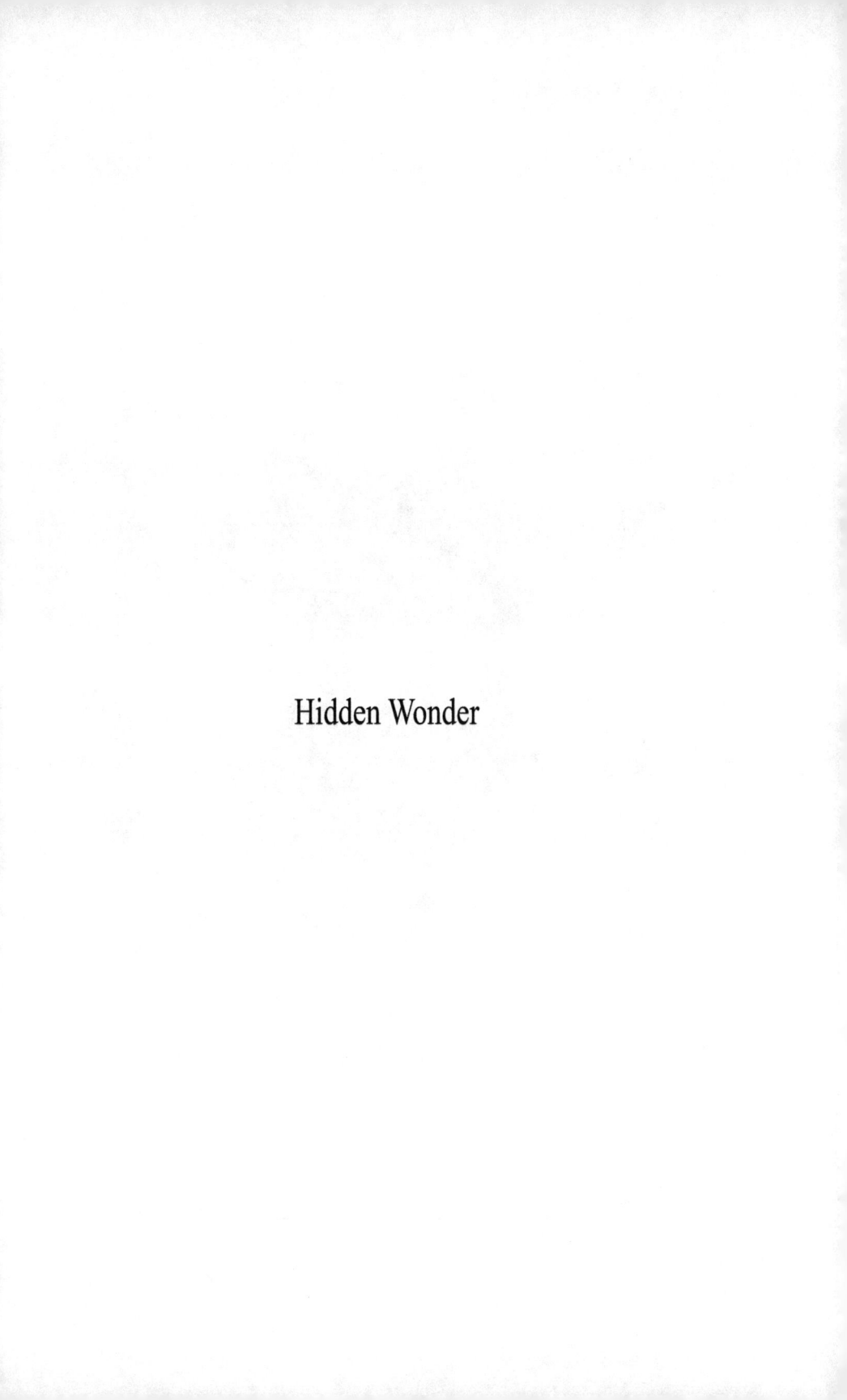

Hidden Wonder

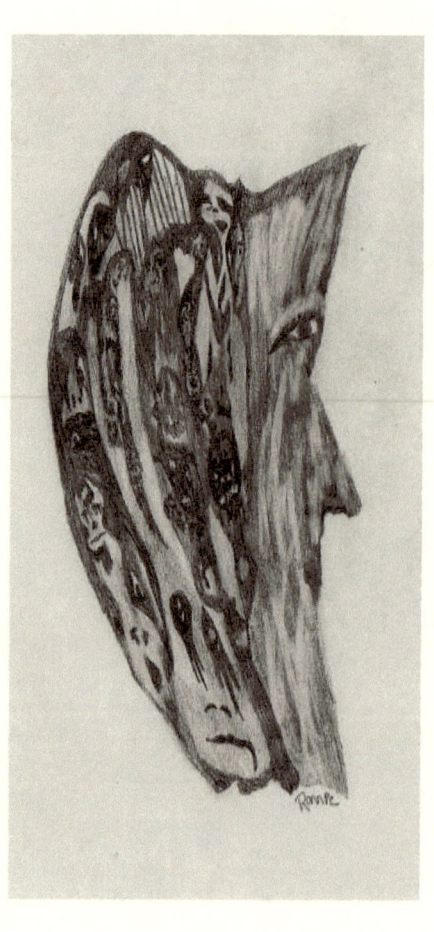

In His Head

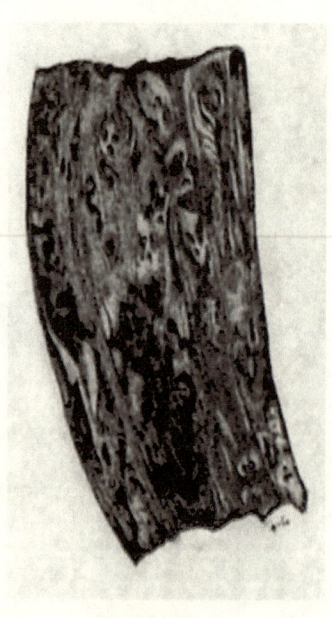

Clouds of Color

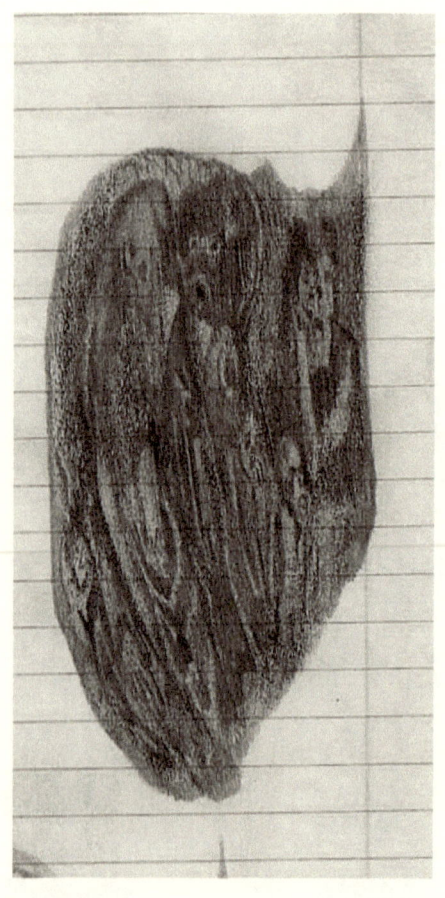

Reflections In Blue

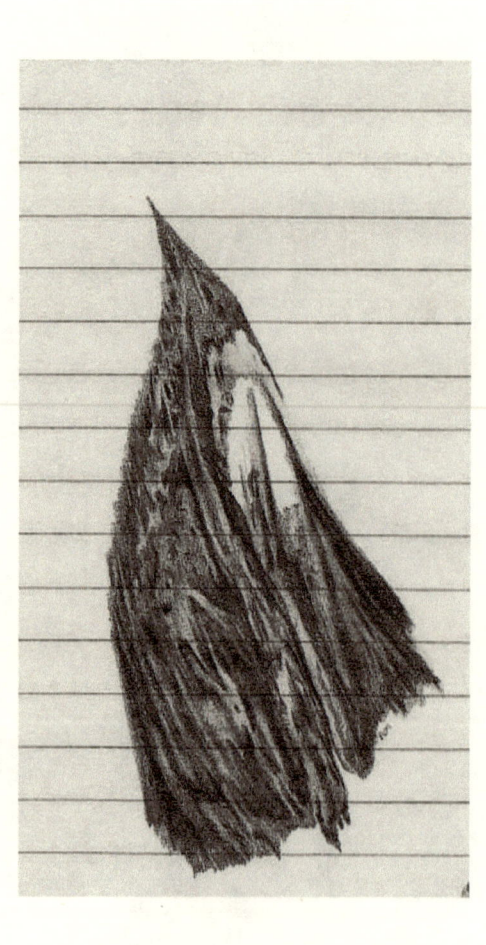

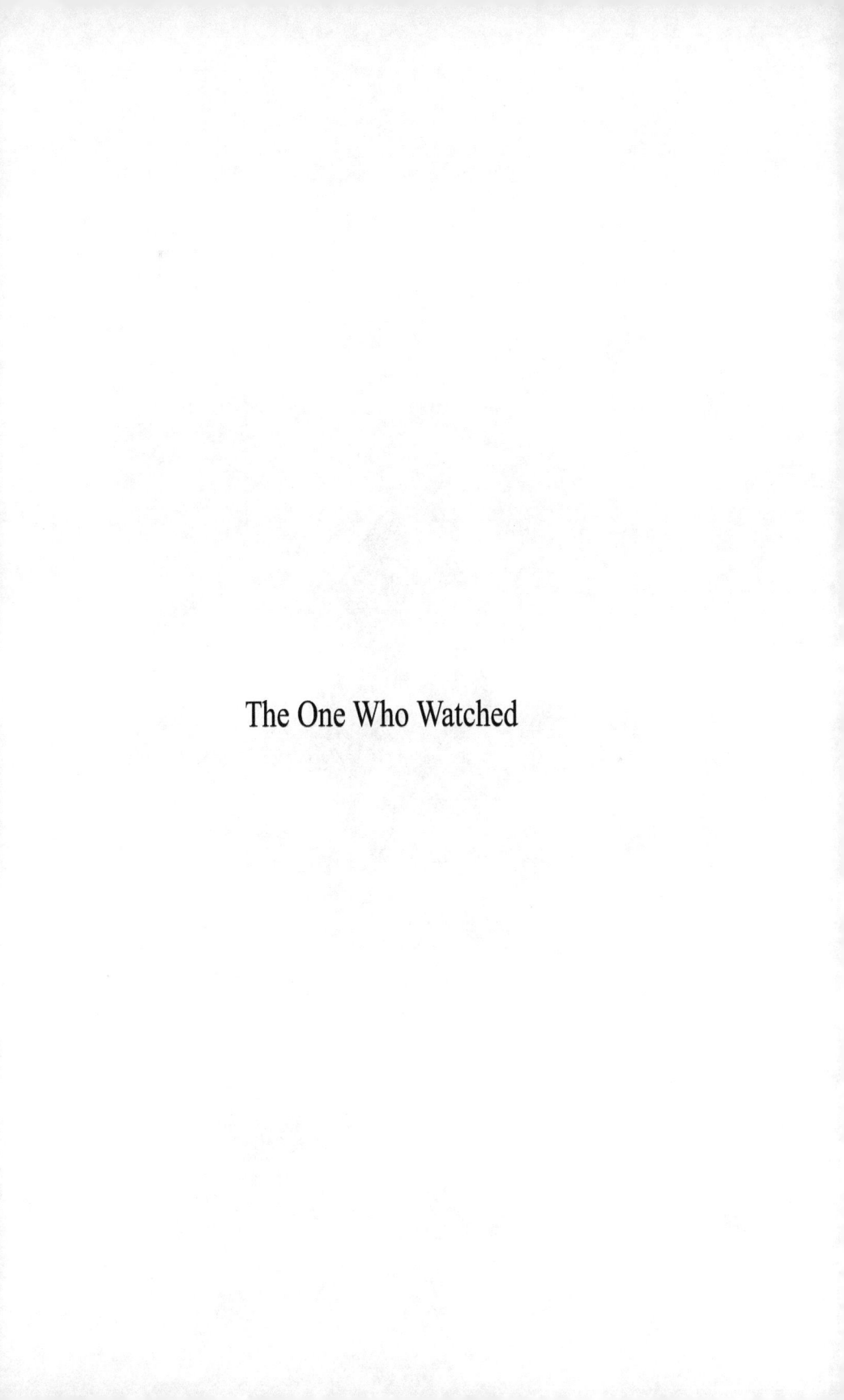

The One Who Watched

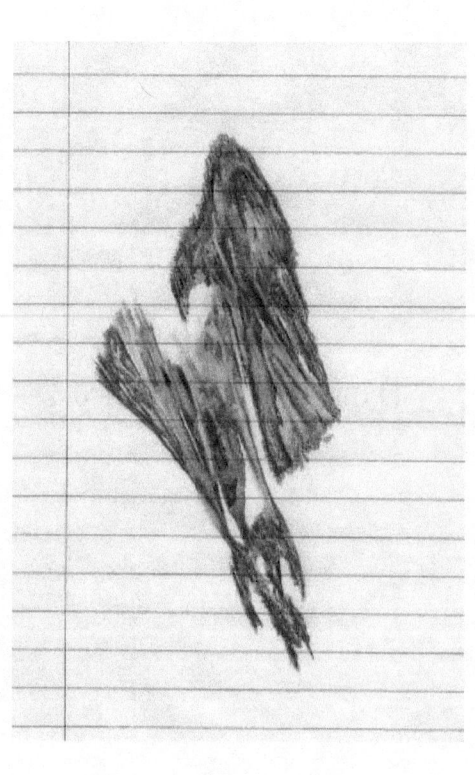

Porky Gets Scared

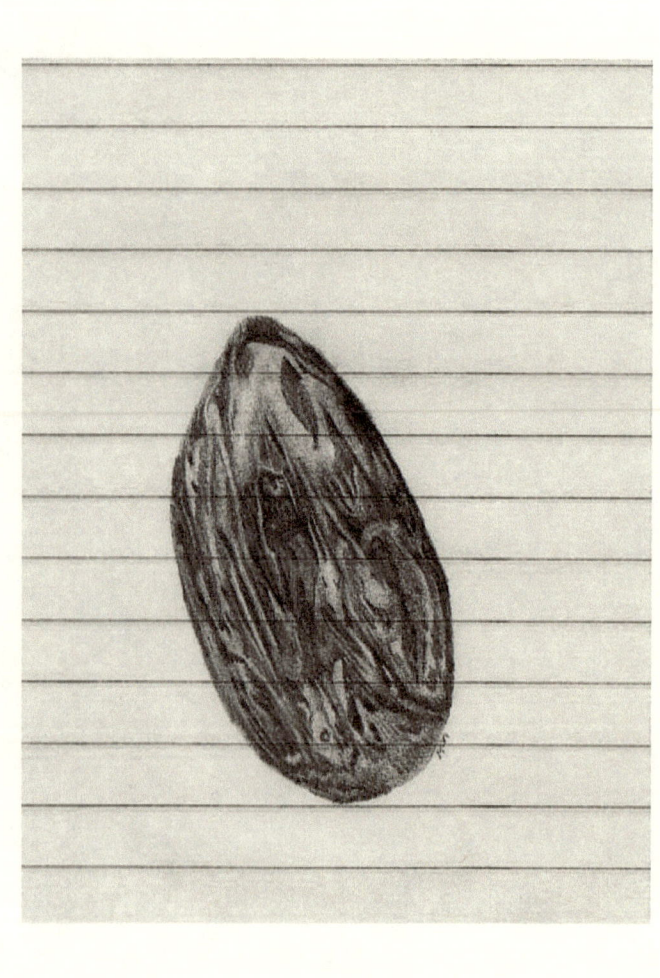

Looking Glass

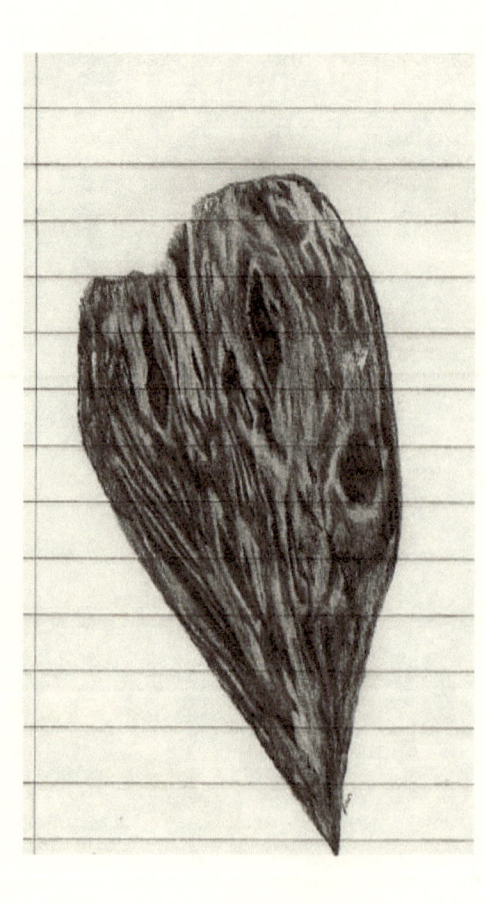

Full Speed

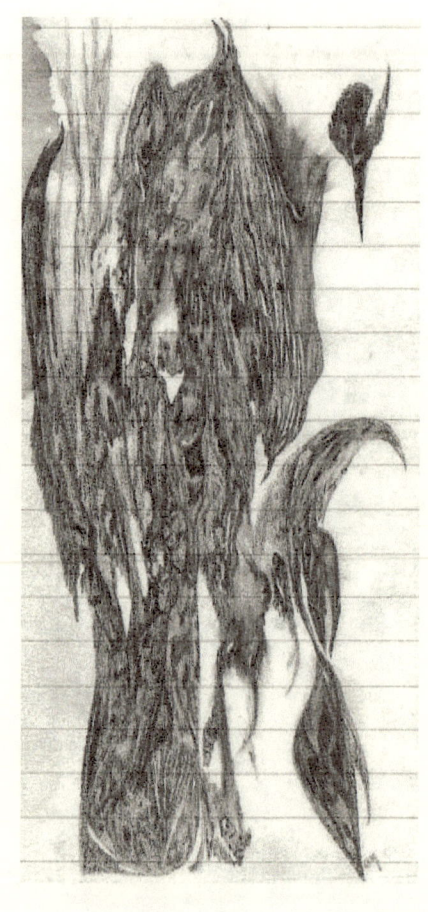

On The Wings Of A Dragon

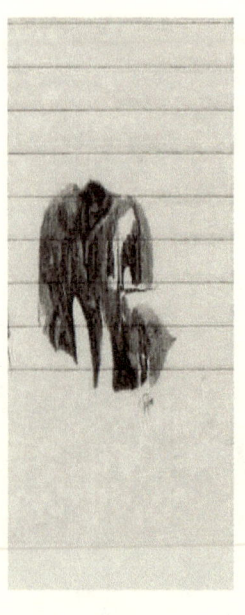

An Angel

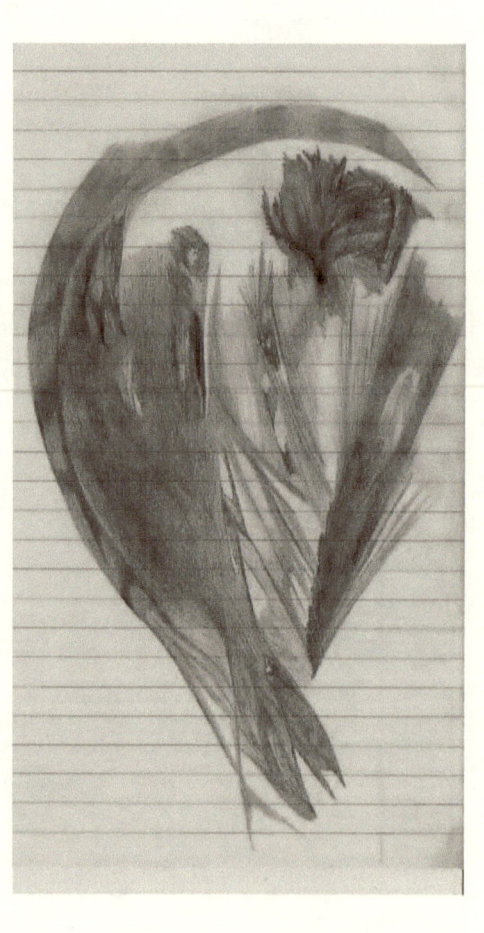

Native Feather

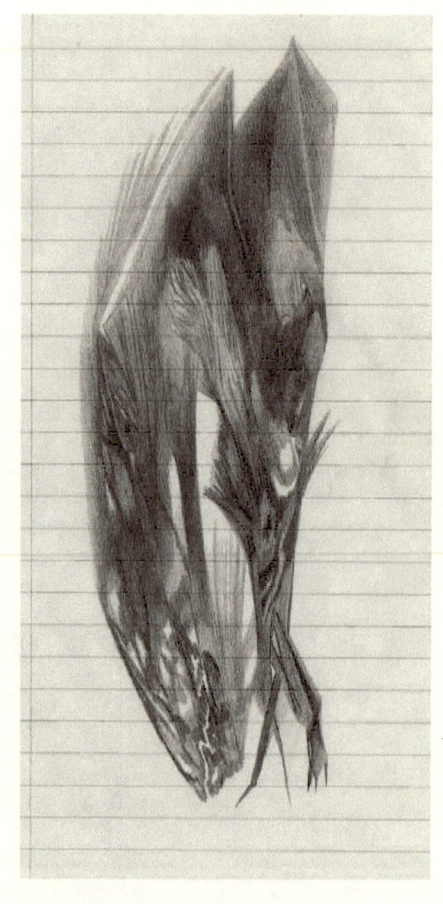

Witch Doctor

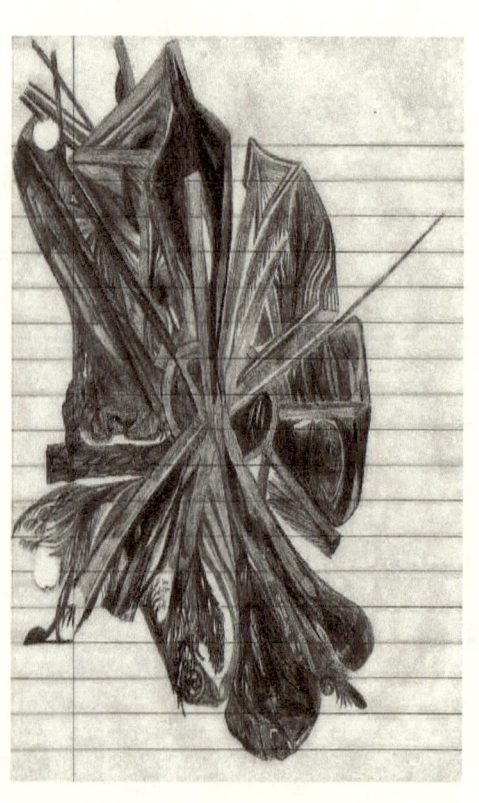

The Puzzle Picture

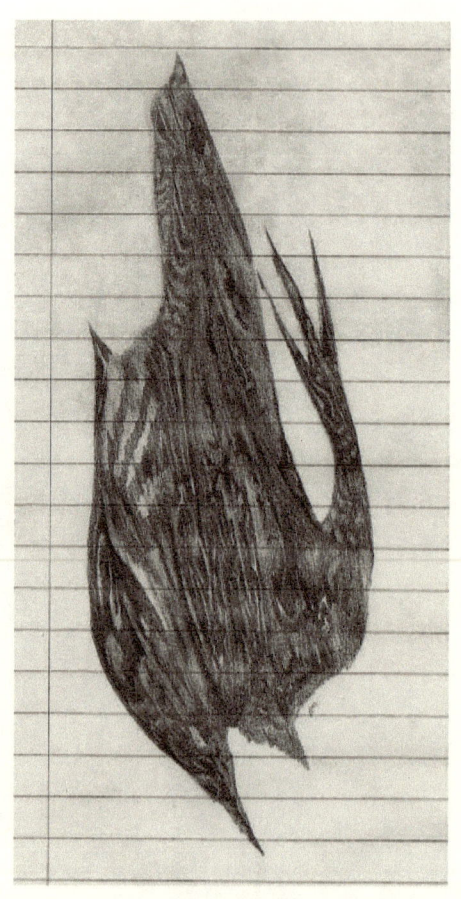

Alien Three

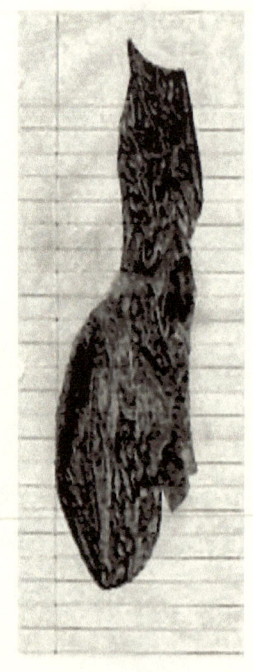

The Cat

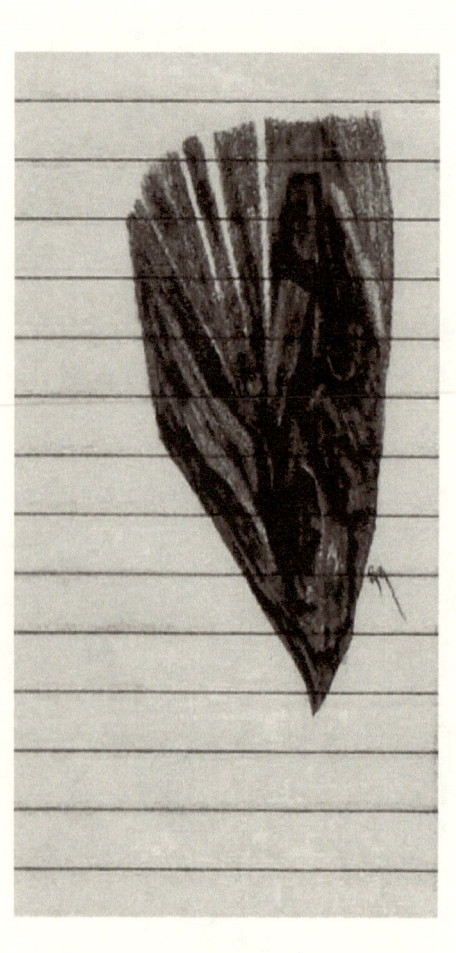

The Knife Cut

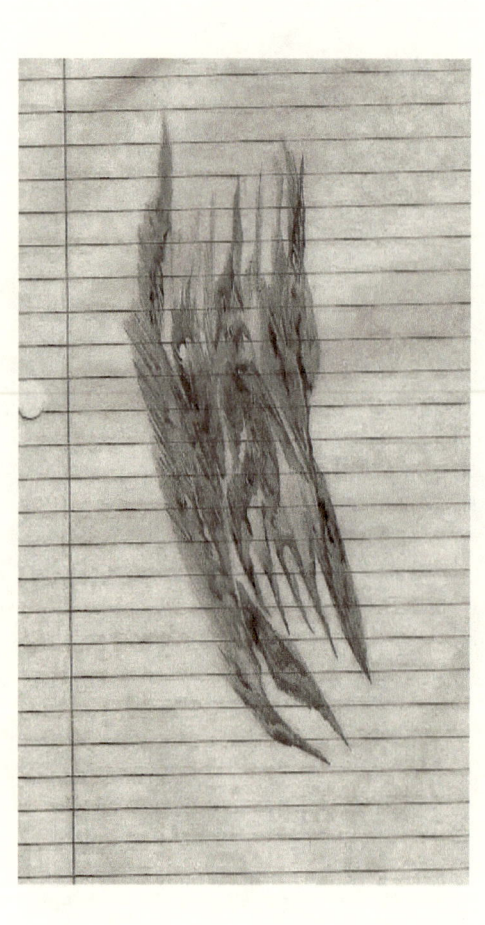

Feathered Dragon

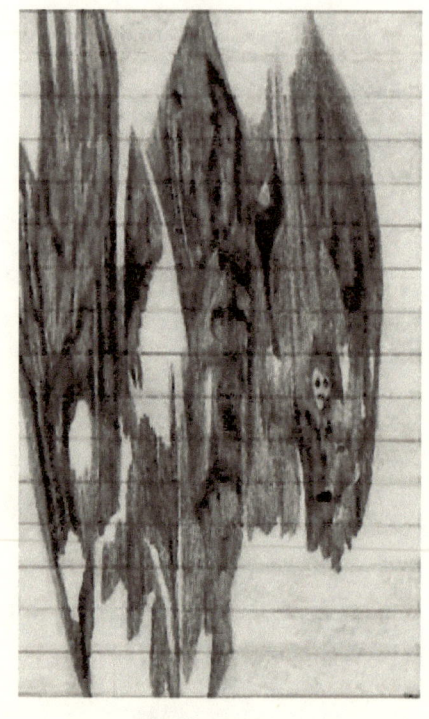

Hidden In Darkness

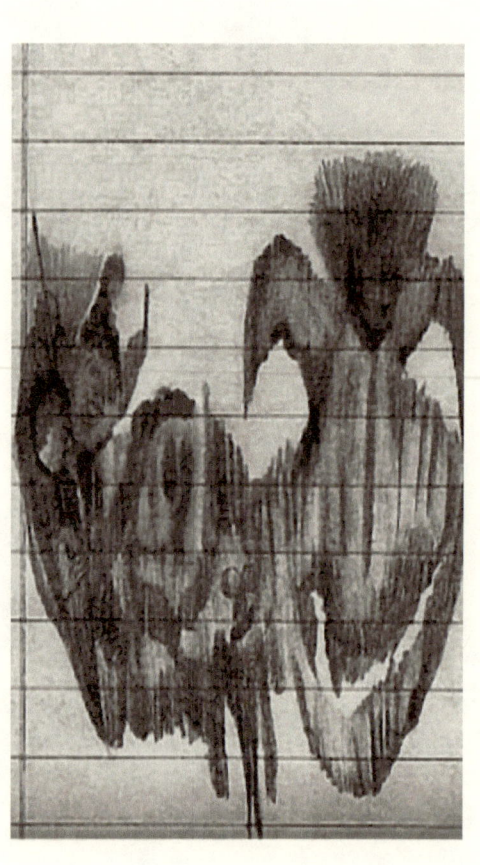

Comedy Vs. Tragedy

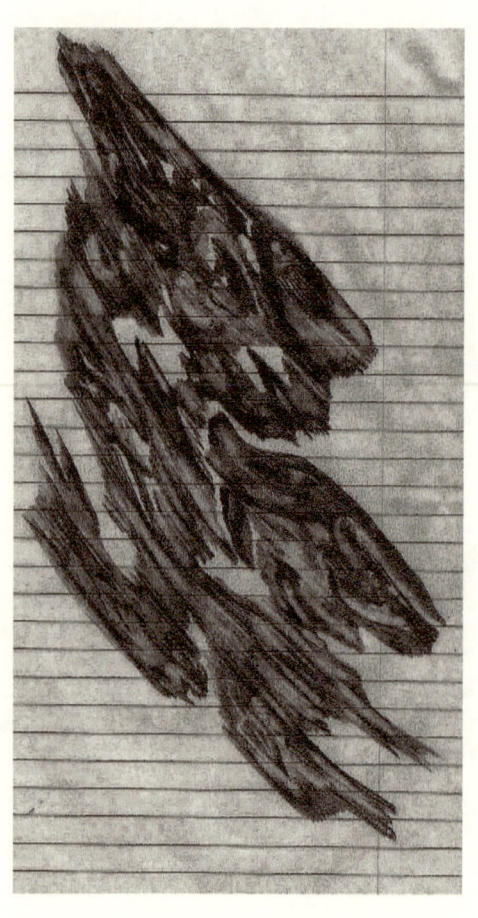

Extra Terrestrial

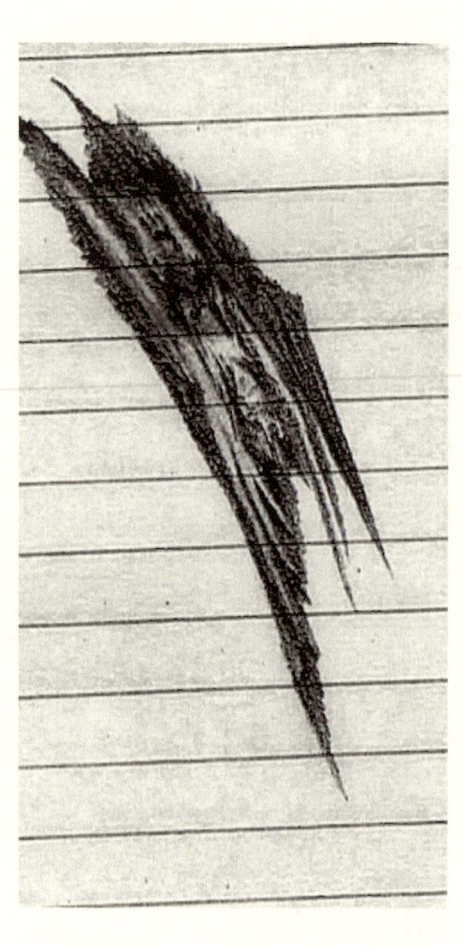

Queen Of The Butterflies

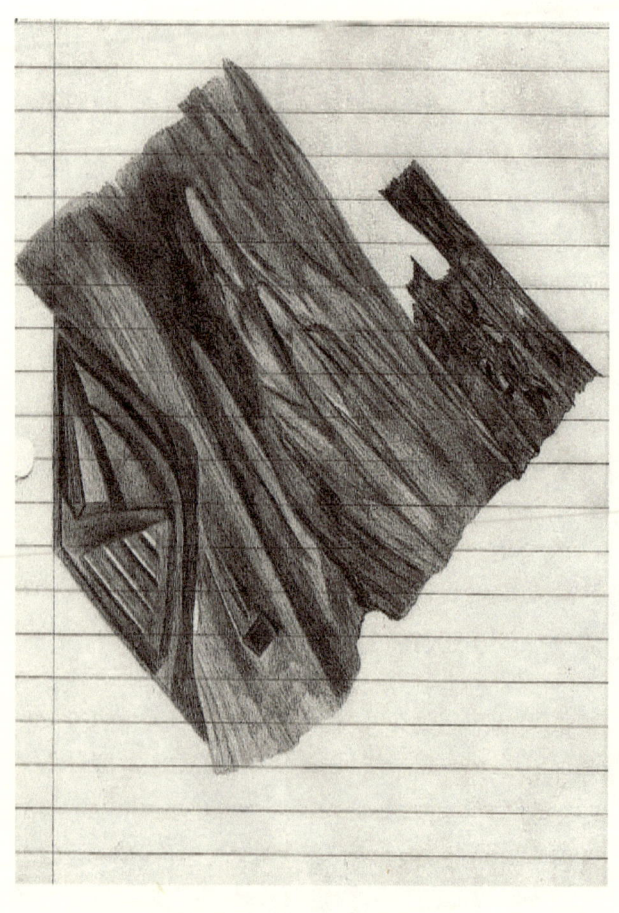

Lost Images of a Family

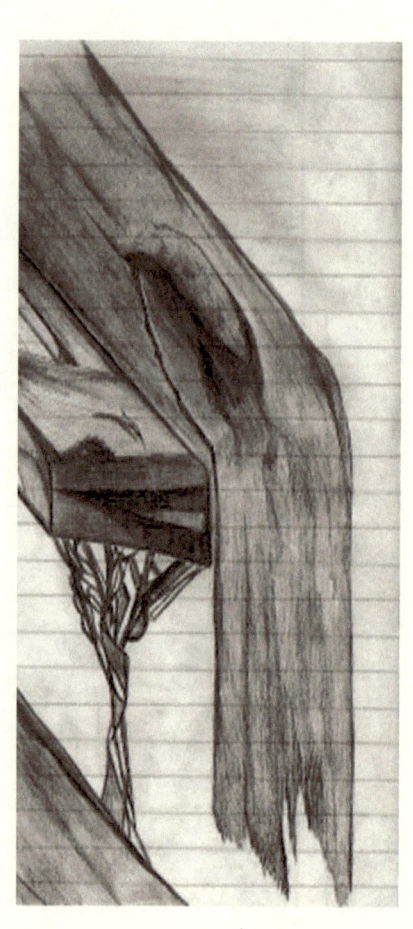

Wood Melting

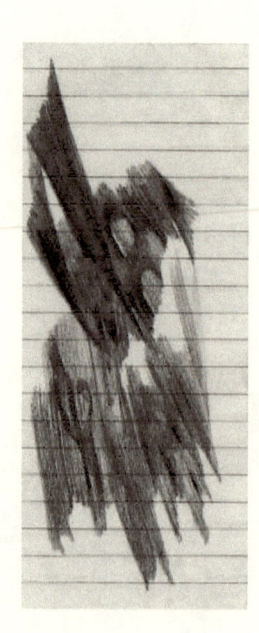

Hung

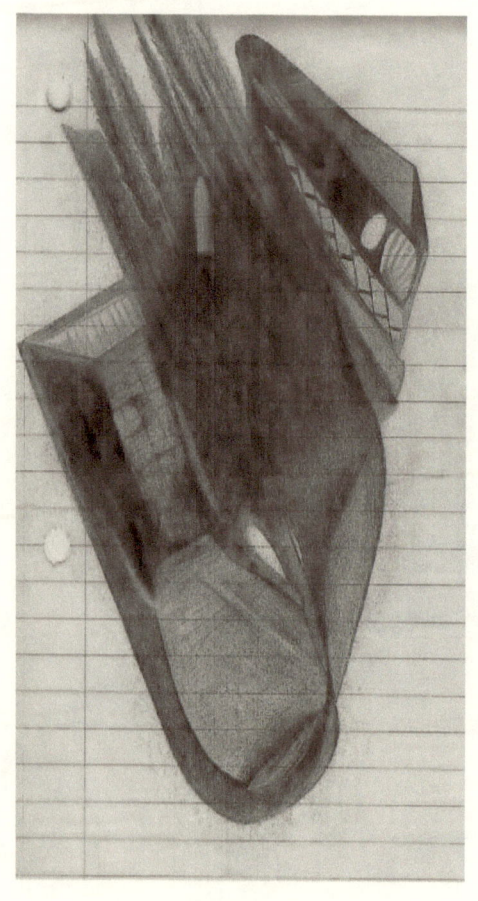

Oppression

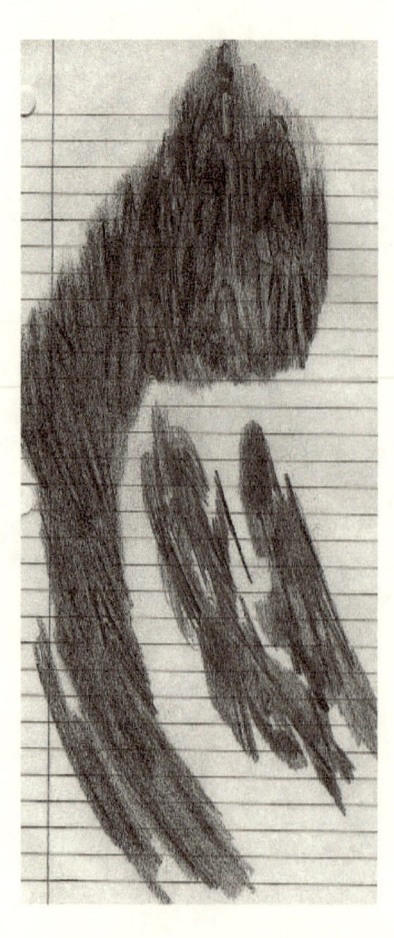

The Shaman

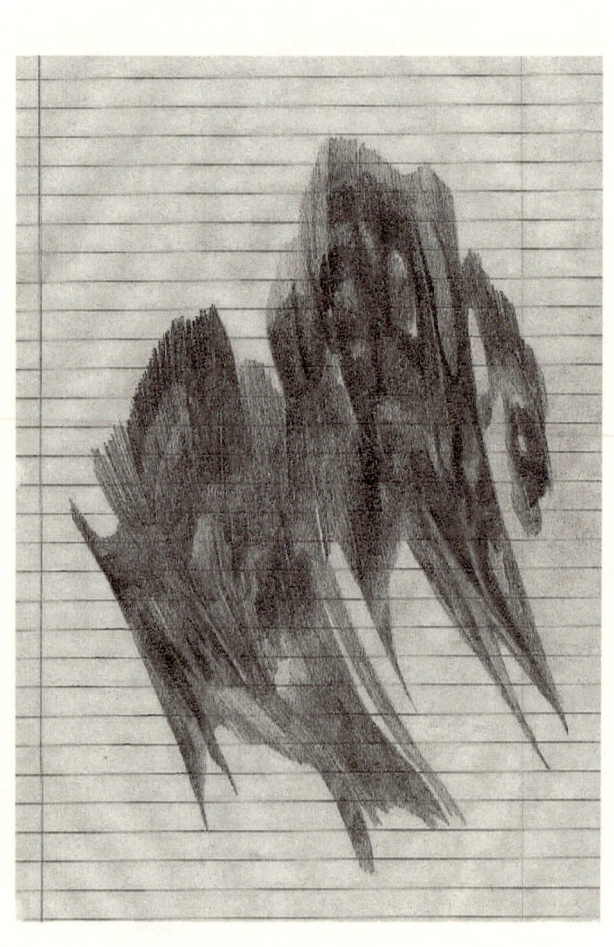

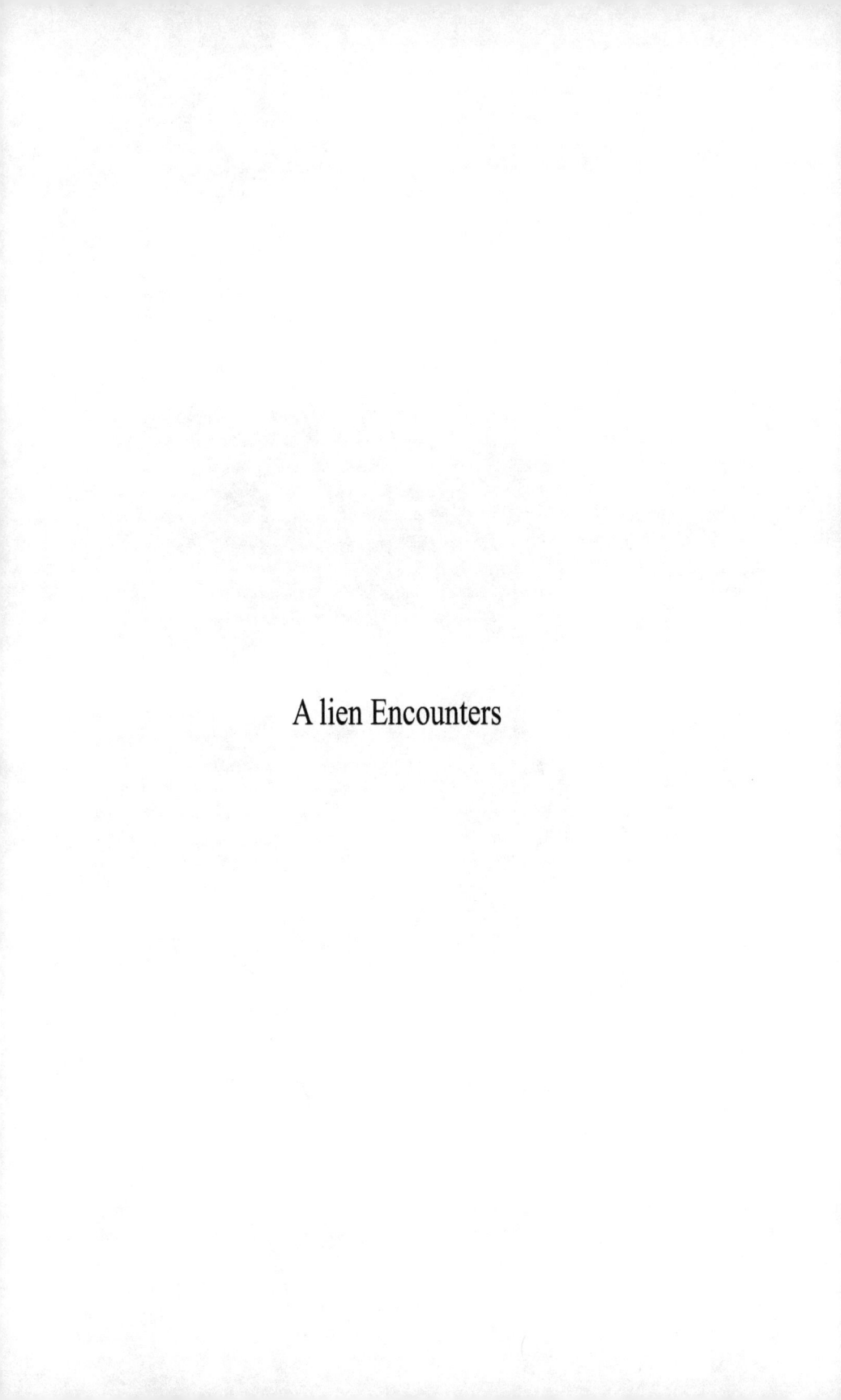

A lien Encounters

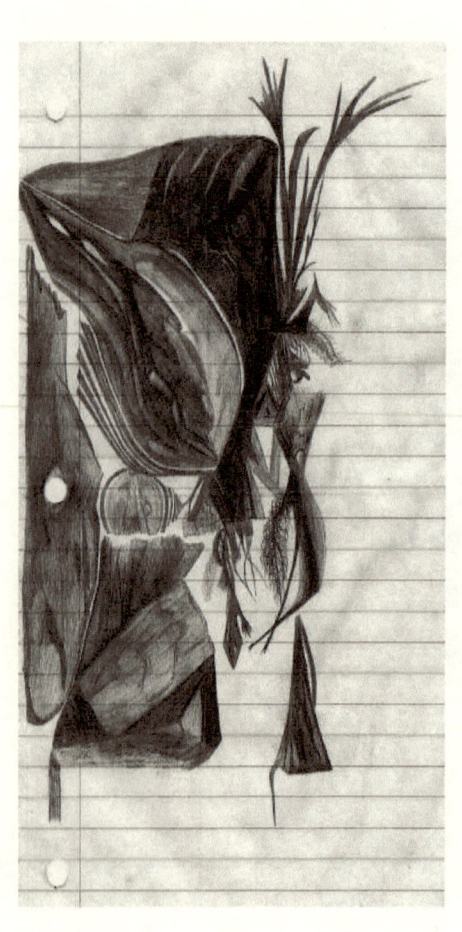

The Swamp

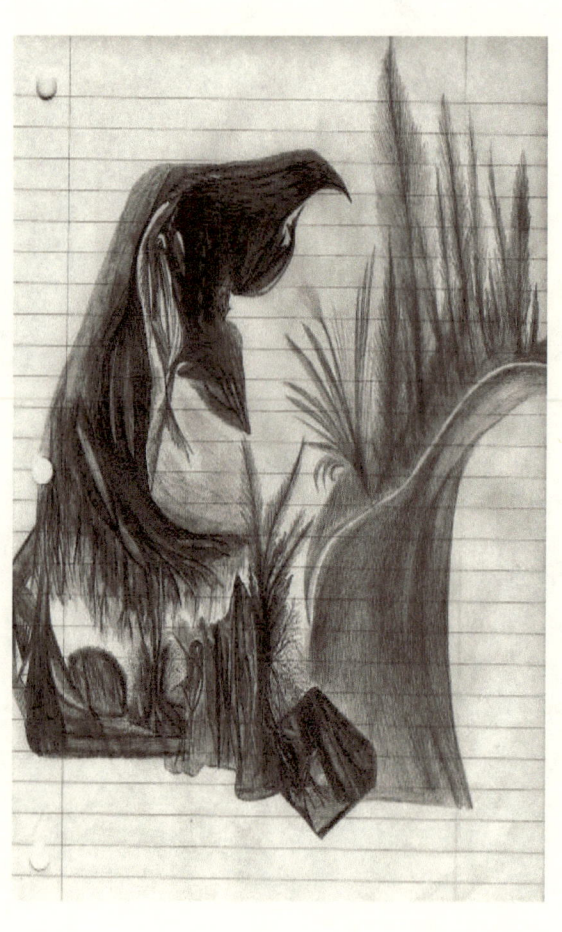

A Crow

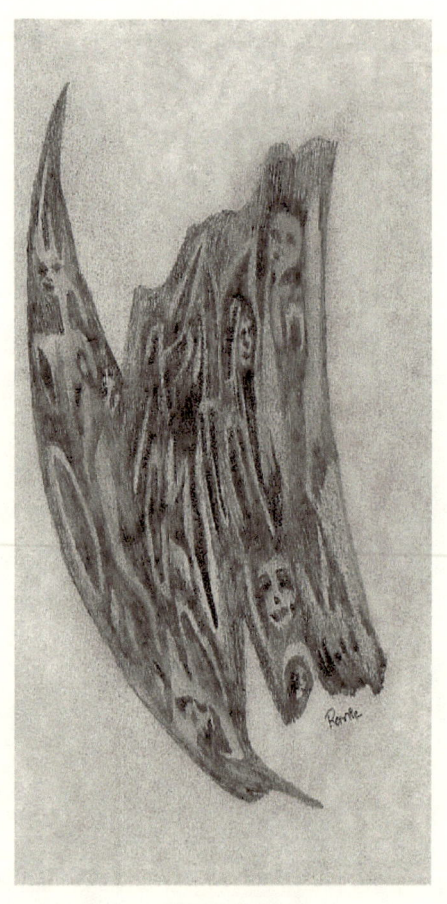

Hallow Looks

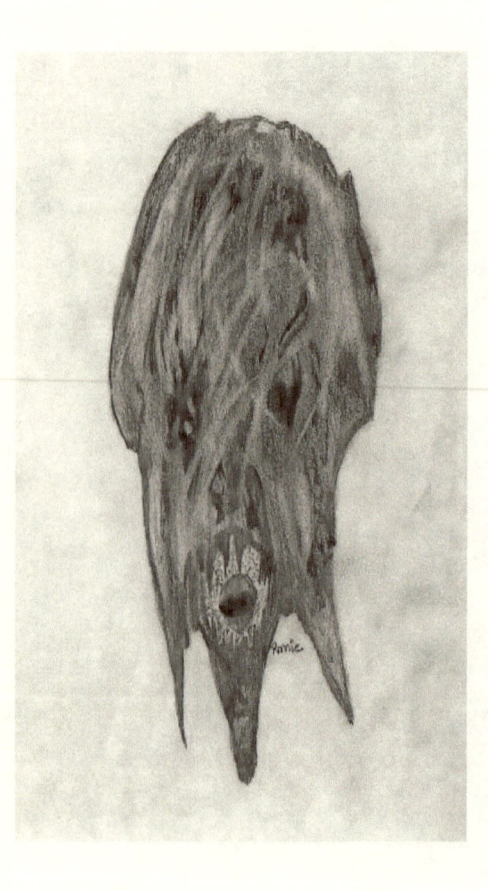

Looking Out

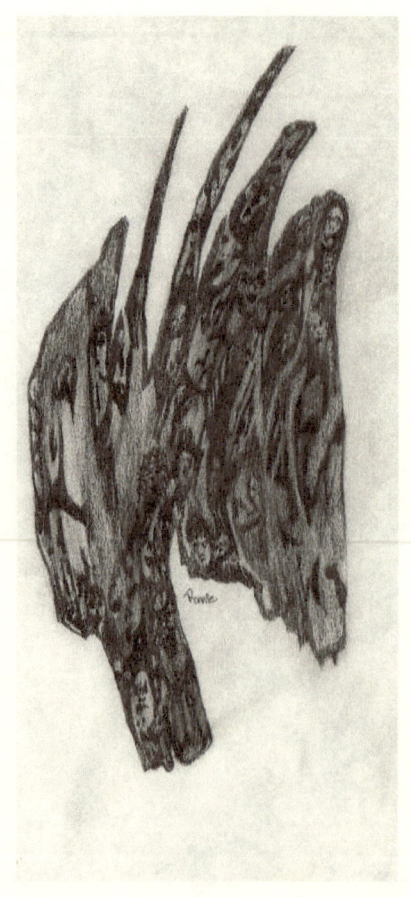

Butterfly Dreams

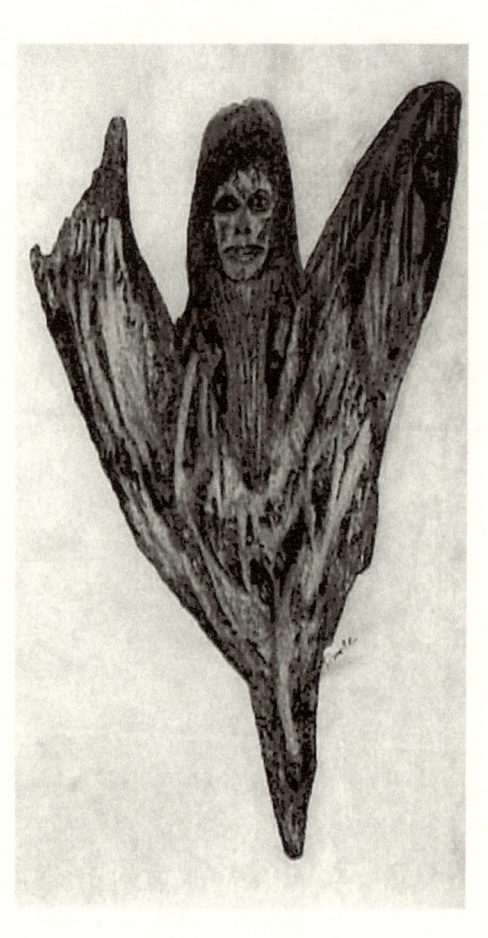

The Moth

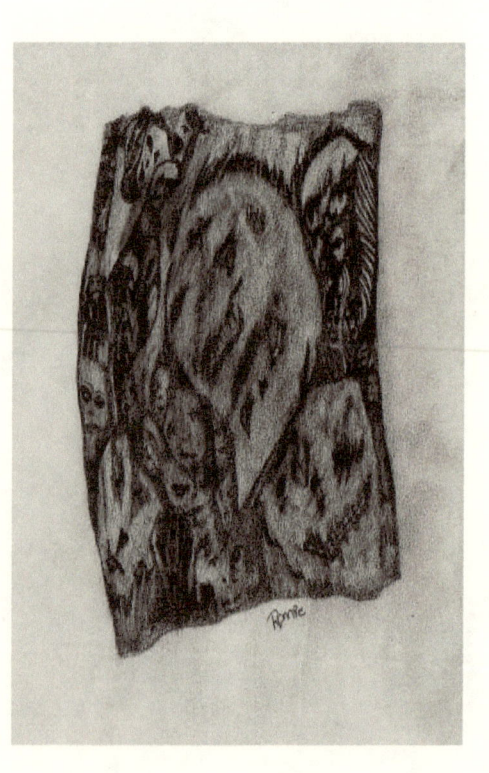

Zombie Dreams

Artists Note

I hope you have enjoyed this book of art. If you have gleaned a few secrets then all the better. I set out to show the shape of dreams and the surreal, the subconscious and the fantasy realms of shadow. If I have succeeded in entertaining your imagination the world is as it should be I hope. These are just representations of those things that I can not put into the written word. At any rate I wish you well until next time.

Ron Koppelberger Jr. December 2012